GET OUT OF
THE TRUCK!

GET OUT OF THE TRUCK!

Build the business you always dreamed about

IDAN SHPIZEAR

Get out of the truck!
Build the business you always dreamed about

Copyright © 2020 Idan Shpizear

website

ISBN

First Edition

Editor:
Cover image:
Cover and interior design: Adina Cucicov

Contents

Introduction

Let me begin by telling you what this book is *not*. This is *not* a self-help book of business theory written by a guy who has worn ties to work since his very first job.

I was not born into business. My path to success did not pass through the halls of Stanford. I do not have an MBA.

What I *do* have is one of the fastest growing franchises in the United States. And when I started that company, all I had was an $800 Volvo and a two-bedroom apartment I shared with four other guys. Today, 911 Restoration vans are seen parked outside distressed properties all across North America. I built that business from almost nothing. And *that* experience is why I can give you the guidance no one else can.

I can show you the way forward because I know a thing or two about where you've been.

I grew up learning to work with my hands. My father owned a farm in Israel, and I spent my youth digging in the dirt, tending and harvesting vegetables alongside my dad. But I always dreamed of building a legacy of my own.

After serving in the military, I moved to the United States in hot pursuit of the American Dream. Like many aspiring business owners, I underestimated the challenges that lay between me and the success I was chasing. I thought that to move to America was to have it made. Instead, I had to struggle, scrimp, and save. I took a job for a carpet cleaning company and ate most of my meals at MacDonald's, hanging on to my cups between visits so I could get free refills. I slept on the floor because I couldn't buy a bed. I saved every penny I could, I learned as much as possible about the industry I worked in, and when I had enough cash squirreled way, I made my boss an offer on his own company.

Just like that, I had gone from a tradesman to a businessman. And I quickly learned that in order to make it work, I'd have to transform my mindset as well as my job title.

I am about to share every essential lesson that helped me "get out of the truck" both physically and mentally so I could fulfill my dream. The guidance I offer you isn't just about business philosophy. It's about navigating a transformation. This book is for every tradesperson who dreams of building their own legacy . . . for the men and women who are used to thinking about skilled, quality workmanship more than business strategy. You may feel lost. You may feel like you're in over your head.

But whether you're an aspiring entrepreneur or you already own a business, there's something I want you to know:

> You've already given yourself an incredible opportunity just by taking control of your own professional trajectory.

While running a business is undeniably challenging—especially at first—it's also the best way to take control of your future. While some brilliant professionals have a long and fulfilling careers in employee positions (and thank goodness for them!), there are others—like you—who are anxious to forge their own path. You see that when you work for someone else, you are at the mercy of their decisions. You can only build wealth if your boss does. You have to set your own standards and objectives according to your employer's standards and objectives.

As a business owner, you break free from the limits imposed on you by someone else's vision. You decide how much money you make, how quickly your business grows, and what kind of reputation you want for your brand.

That's the good news. Here's the bad news.

Less than 2% of businesses survive their first three years. A whopping 85% of new companies close in the first 12 months.

With statistics like that, it may seem like the odds are against you. But the truth is, they're not.

Not if you take control of your future and make the changes you need to make to transition from a tradesperson to a business person.

I've seen a lot of new business owners transition from the truck to the office without making any changes to their mentality, and this is a recipe for failure. They don't learn to think like an entrepreneur, and as a result, they wind up making decisions reactively instead of strategically. I've seen business owners make mistakes such as:

- Starting a business before understanding what it takes to succeed.
- Making business decisions based on feelings only.
- Hiring the wrong people for the right job or hiring the right people for the wrong job.
- Clinging to a "my way or the highway" mentality that makes them resistant to adopting new and essential tools.
- Refusing to take full responsibility and blaming *someone else* for their failures.

I wrote this book to help you avoid errors like these . . . errors that can destroy a new business and your great potential for growth. In these pages, you won't find the magic key to overnight success. What you will find are insights on the most important elements for building a successful business. Work on mastering these key aspects of owning a business, and you'll gradually transform both your company and yourself for the better.

The principles in this book come from my own hard-earned wisdom as I transitioned from a carpet cleaner to the founder and CEO of a nationwide company. I've also drawn from my experience mentoring the franchisees who have helped 911 Restoration has become one of the fastest growing franchises in the United States.

While I recommend reading this book cover-to-cover so you have an understanding of the bigger picture, this guide is also designed for easy reference, so you can pinpoint your area of struggle, flip to that section, and determine where your weaknesses are and how you can move beyond them.

Whether you choose to read this book from beginning to end or you simply pick and choose the sections that feel most relevant to your current needs, I ask that you always remember one thing:

> If you want to grow a thriving business,
> **you must strive for progress, not perfection.**

There is no such thing as perfection in business. There is no perfect product, no perfect company, no clear-cut finish line. Every day, the culture evolves, your customers' needs change, the competition progresses, and technology advances. Today's "perfect product" will not be the same as tomorrow's perfect product. So stop obsessing over an elusive end goal. There is no end in business.

Your success as an entrepreneur depends on your willingness to adapt and respond to changing customer needs. It depends on your ability to work quickly and take decisive action towards meaningful progress. To flourish, you must turn your attention to forward motion, always asking yourself, "What action can I take in this moment to improve myself or my company?"

> In fact, consider these your three mantras for success:
>
> - Progress over perfection.
> - Self-awareness is the key to change.
> - Set clear goals.

My goal in writing this book is to get you started in your business the right way . . . or even just get you out of the truck. I believe every human being has unlimited potential, and my hope is to help you discover your own with this short, straight-forward guide to running a thriving business.

Because there is no doubt in my mind that you can do it.

CHAPTER 1

Why Are You Going into the Business?

Before you do anything else—before you draw up your business plan or start researching the competition—make sure you know why you want to open a business in the first place.

This may seem so simple. You may even be tempted to breeze right past this chapter. But stick around. A lot of businesses fall apart because an entrepreneur didn't connect their efforts to a core passion, and they didn't set a clear vision for the journey from Point A to Point B.

On the flip side, if your dream is rooted in personal conviction, a mission, and a practical plan, there's no reason you can't find the success you want.

Find Your Passion in the Work

So, why do you want to build a business? Is it because:

- You're following in the footsteps of a parent?
- You see a great opportunity to make a profit in this field?
- It's your passion?

Any one of those responses is fine. It's okay to want to build wealth, and it's okay to want to carry on the family legacy.

What's not okay is committing to the huge responsibility of creating a business without first discovering the passion that's going to fuel your career. Building a business is extremely difficult work, and when the going gets tough, you will quickly find that "My dad did this job" or "I want to be able to afford expensive vacations" will not be enough to keep you motivated.

So, even if your initial reason for starting a business is something other than "It's my driving passion," you need to sit down and find out what your real passion is and how it's going to play out in your business. For example:

- Do you love serving your community?
- Are you energized by the thought of leading a team and mentoring young professionals?
- Can you identify the deeper service you provide?

As I built 911 Restoration, I was most passionate about having the opportunity to help people in distress rebuild their homes and businesses. Disaster would strike and we'd be there to guide families and individuals through some of the darkest chapters in their life, giving them a new beginning on the other side.

Take the time to find a passion like that within your own business.

Lay Out Your Vision and Mission

Where is your business headed? How will you be defining success and what role do you want your company to play in the larger community?

These questions are important to answer, because they guide the choices you make going forward and they serve as a constant reminder of why you are doing this in the first place. Remember, owning a business is about taking control of your own future. So before you dive in, take time to determine:

- What your business will look like in 5, 10, 20 years.
- What type of people you want to have on your team.
- What is most important to you. How do you define success on a deeper level?

Once you know these things, it's time to figure out how you're going to make it happen.

Know How You Are Going to Win

Now you've figured out why you want to start a business. The next step is to figure out why *you* are the person to do it . . . why *this company* is going to succeed.

How are you going to reach these goals? What assets do you personally bring to your industry? What can you do to set your business apart from your competitors?

Think about things like:

- **Marketing:** What strategies will you use to grow your business? Who has the expertise to help you create an effective marketing campaign?
- **Customer Service:** What can you offer customers that they may not be getting from your competitors? What extra steps might make them feel valued?
- **Unique Product:** What service, product, or experience can you offer that's new? Is there any problem your customers have that other businesses are not addressing? How can you go above and beyond?

Give yourself time to brainstorm. If you're currently working for another business in the same industry, use this opportunity to pay close attention to what works and what doesn't. Notice how customers react to the service they receive. Listen to their comments or complaints.

IN SHORT

- Know why you want to build a business.
- Know the end result you're working towards.
- Know how you're going to get there.

CHAPTER 2

Are You Ready and Willing to Build a Business?

One of the hardest questions you have to ask yourself as you start your own business is whether you're actually ready and willing to build a business.

It's easy to mistake passion and enthusiasm for readiness and commitment. But building a business—actually taking the steps necessary to grow and increase profits—requires more practical commitments.

It's like making the choice to eat healthy or get fit. I might feel inspired by a friend who goes to the gym every day. I might feel motivated reading an article on healthy eating practices. But real commitment means there has to be an actual change in the content of my grocery cart. It means investing in organic vegetables and setting aside time for exercise.

The same is true for your business. It's not enough to feel energized. You must be willing to commit in concrete ways.

Prepare yourself by asking these important questions:

What part are you going to play in the business?

A lot of business owners don't realize that the term "owner" doesn't really clarify a specific role. Neither does the term "boss." Likewise, "being in charge" is not a real job description.

A successful entrepreneur goes into business ownership knowing exactly what skills he or she brings to the table, as well as what weaknesses. Do you have outstanding people skills? You might focus most of your energy on building relationships and overseeing customer service. Are you exceptionally skilled in your field? Maybe your focus should be on training and perfecting services while you allow a manager to oversee the interpersonal aspects of the job.

Or perhaps you have an incredible gift for business strategy, in which case you may be the kind of business owner who focuses their time in the office or boardroom.

No matter who you are or what you have to offer, have an honest conversation with yourself about how you can best serve the company. Then, fully commit to that role. Be open to bringing on extra help if there are areas where you fall short. Remember, you do not need to be good at everything. You just need to be really good (or even great) at *something* and actively look for ways to use that strength to your company's advantage.

And—this is important—be humble enough to learn so you can at least build competency in your areas of weakness.

That brings me to the next question:

How are you going to continue developing your skills and character?

The success of your business depends on your willingness to grow. It's up to you to master new skills, keep up with an evolving industry, and seek self-improvement opportunities to ensure you are an effective leader and an empowered entrepreneur.

You may be thinking, "No problem! I'm always happy to learn!" But in order to really commit to personal development, you must make a plan today. How are you going to hold yourself accountable? What will you do to make sure you're always learning?

In my own development as an entrepreneur, I quickly learned that a growth mindset was key to building a promising career and a thriving business.

Here are some things you can do to cultivate that mindset, just as I did:

- Adopt the belief that everything *can* change, including you. If you're not satisfied with your current situation, you have the ability to create transformation.
- Write down who you want to become and what you want to create in your life so you can move forward with a clear focus.
- Start creating small changes in your life. Start with minor adjustments like getting up earlier . . . changes that are guaranteed to be successful.
- Find mentors that can and will help you grow.
- Identify the ways in which you want to grow, then hang out with people who are more skilled in those areas.
- Plan to spend one hour a day learning about the latest innovations in your field.
- Commit to attending specific conventions and trade shows.
- Create a system for open communication between you and your employees so you can hear their feedback.
- Make a habit of shadowing your employees and managers to learn more about their skill set and how their work affects the business.

In other words, be open to learning opportunities and stay curious about the latest advancements in your field. The better you become as both a professional and a person, the stronger your business will be.

Work on making these small changes little by little every day. And if you miss a day, simply forgive yourself and get right back into the routine. Growth can and should be fun, so think of being your own cheerleader rather than a taskmaster.

Which areas of the business will you need help with?

If you want your business to thrive, you need to go in with a realistic understanding of your own abilities. While I stand by my statement that you are a human being with limitless possibilities, I also need you to know that "limitless" is not the same thing as "perfect." We all have shortcomings. And your ability to achieve great things depends on your willingness to acknowledge those shortcomings immediately.

Ask yourself which areas of the business present the highest challenge for you. Then, once you've pinpointed those areas of weakness, think about how you're going to get help navigating those areas.

There are two major avenues for finding expert assistance.

1. **Hiring.** Determine not only which roles you need to fill, but the skills you should look for in your employees in order to make sure you get the exact help you need. For example, let's say you're hiring a manager. You might know a guy who's an incredible tradesman, but if that's your area of strength, you have more to gain by seeking a manager who is great at closing leads. That way, both

skills are covered by those in leadership positions, and both you and your manager have the opportunity to learn from one another.

2. **Self-development.** This goes back to the second point above. Seek out opportunities to build skills in your areas of challenge. Keep your eyes open for professionals who are particularly good at the aspects of business ownership that present some struggle for you. Invite them out for coffee so you can pick their brains. Use this book to discover new opportunities to improve.

IN SHORT

- Lean into your own talents.
- Make a concrete plan for personal growth and improvement.
- Seek whatever help you need to make sure there are no weak links in your business.

CHAPTER 3

What Do You Know About the Industry and Your Potential for Success?

S o now you have a clear grasp on why you're starting your own business and what objectives will keep you motivated through the tough times. You've done the work to learn what you need to learn about yourself. Now it's time to make sure you know the industry just as well.

Keep in mind that knowing the industry is not the same as knowing the trade. In fact, if you're reading this book because you're trying to keep your business alive, you might be surprised to discover that some of your best solutions lie in this chapter. That is to say, you might find that you don't know your business as well as you think you do, because you've only ever known one side of it—the trade side.

A lot of tradespeople become business people with total confidence that they can succeed because they know what it takes to provide expert service. They know plumbing or roofing or fire restoration inside out. The problem is, running a business requires an entirely different set of skills, and to do it well, you have to see the industry from an entirely different perspective.

Whether you're just now starting your business or you're trying to resuscitate a struggling company, here are the details you should know.

Know the Size of the Market

First, ask yourself how big you want your business to be. What amount of success will make opening a business worth it? Are you hoping to one day expand? Do you dream of opening new locations across the city, state, or even the country?

Nail down your goals, then determine what it's going to take for you to reach them. In order to realistically calculate your potential for success, you need to know:

1. What you're up against.
2. The degree to which your services are needed.

In order to answer these questions, you need to research the market. Ask:

- *How high is the local demand for services like mine? Will I find enough buyers in this area?*
- *What's the competition like? How many other businesses will I be competing with?*
- *Between the local population, the demand for service, and my competitors, what potential challenges and advantages do I face as I open a new business?*

Once you know what you're up against, move onto the next important question:

> *How are you going to compete?*

Know the Competition

Sometimes entrepreneurs get so focused on what they're doing to stay competitive that they forget to notice what The Other Guy is doing to stay competitive.

Huge mistake.

You learn so much from watching your competitors. Not only do you discover what you need to do to keep up and excel, but when you observe your competitors' methods, successes, and missteps, you get clues about what works in your industry. And this is never more important than when you're first establishing your business.

It's also imperative that you study your competitors to find out how you can set yourself apart. Notice what they do to succeed, but also think about what they're not doing . . . how you can differentiate your company, forge a new path, and become a market leader rather than a follower.

A great example is Ruby's Shake Shack in Newport. If you've never been, it's basically a burger joint on the beach. The food is fine. Not exceptional, but it does the job. So how does a not-exceptional burger joint thrive in a world already jam-packed with burger joints? Location and atmosphere. The view at the Crystal Cove Shake Shack is unreal, and customers come there to enjoy the California-casual beach vibe. This is what sets the business apart and makes it a popular dining option.

So, when you're checking out the competition, think about what you can do differently to stand out from the crowd.

Research the competition to find out:

- How they get clients
- How they established themselves in this market—Did they build a strong brand? Are they great at generating leads?
- Where their marketing efforts are falling flat

- What feedback they get in online reviews
- How your business stands out against theirs
- What you can do to offer your customers something they won't get from your competitors

The answers to these questions provide a solid foundation as you build a strategy for staying competitive.

Know What It Means to Make a Profit in This Business

You've already figured out what success means to you. Now you have to understand what it takes to achieve that success. And I'm not talking about what it takes in terms of drive, creativity, and strategy. I'm talking about cold, hard numbers. Look at:

- What it costs to operate your business
- The transaction rates that will help you stay competitive in the market
- Your profit margin based on the previous two figures

Based on those figures, how many jobs do you need to do to reach your profit goal this year? How does that break down into quarterly goals? Monthly goals?

Now, let's say you break it down into monthly goals and find yourself thinking, "That's impossible! No way can we do x jobs every month!"

Take that reaction as a sign that something needs to change. Maybe you need to cut costs. Maybe your rates are too low. Maybe it's time to work on generating more leads.

Whatever the problem is, you won't discover it until you sit down, punch the numbers, and determine whether you are *actually* on the right path toward achieving the profits you want.

Know How You're Going to Get Leads

It seems simple, but too many entrepreneurs don't have a clear strategy in place for finding leads. But make no mistake: the very survival of your business depends on your ability to connect with the right customers in the right way at the right time.

And you need to know the most effective methods for generating leads in *your specific industry.* How are customers connecting with businesses like yours?

- Is it through word of mouth? What referral program or incentives can you put in place to encourage people to talk about your business?
- Is it through Internet research? How can you improve your digital marketing strategies for more visibility online?
- Is it through a physical presence in the community? How can you make your storefront more appealing? Are there any community events where you can advertise or set up a booth?

Recognize that not all industries are the same in this regard. Neither are all target markets, for that matter. So rather than relying on a vague idea of how marketing works, make sure you understand how the most successful players in your industry are finding their customers.

Decide How You're Going to Turn Each Job into Another Job

How is "excellence" defined in your field?

If you're going to stand out above the competition, you need to have an answer to this question. You need to be prepared to serve the client better and more completely than anyone else.

Define standard operating procedures now so you and your team are on the same page when you release them to interact with customers. Consider:

- *How can I prepare my employees to do the best possible job?*
- *How can we add value to a standard service?*
- *How do I want customers to feel when we are servicing them?*

Remember that no job is just one job. Every sale or service is an opportunity to generate more business. And the customer service you provide is your brand communicated through the job you perform.

IN SHORT

- Accurately assess the size and demands of the market.
- Study the competition.
- Calculate your potential to make the kind of profits you want to make.
- Create a plan for generating leads.
- Establish set standards for job performance, especially from the perspective of customer service.

CHAPTER 4

What Does Your Business *Actually* Do?

I'll come back to this point many more times over the course of this book, so pay close attention. This idea is one that separates a surviving business from a thriving business.

If you want to be a leader in your industry and inspire long-term customer loyalty, you need to understand what meaningful service your company offers the larger community.

What is a "Meaningful Service?"

By "meaningful service," I'm referring to the way in which you meet a deeper need for your clients.

There are certain professions we already define according to the meaningful service they provide. Consider your child's teacher, for example. You don't think of that person as someone who makes bulletin boards and grades papers; you think of your child's teacher as someone who educates young minds and prepares them for success.

Tradespeople, on the other hand, are often defined by the simple mechanics of what they do. A plumber fixes pipes. A carpet cleaner cleans the carpets. But I can tell you, no matter what physical service you provide, your customers are receiving something much more profound . . . something they need as human beings.

When my partner and I started our restoration business, we learned very quickly that restoration is not just about using fancy equipment to dry houses after a flood. We actually help families and business owners navigate an emotional disaster. Their biggest asset is at risk, and they have no idea how to preserve their property or how they're going to afford it. Our job is to guide them through this disaster with the least amount of pain possible.

I began to relate the challenges our customers faced with my own experience as a business owner. 911 Restoration was *my* biggest asset, and every time I hit a roadblock or a backslide, I had two choices: I could scramble to do some damage control and hope for the best, or I could turn this challenge into a growth opportunity, ultimately coming out of the disaster with an even stronger and more effective business. 911 Restoration has seen growth because our team has chosen to turn every challenge into a Fresh Start, and that has become our driving philosophy in serving customers. When people call our technicians for help, they don't just get water extraction or smoke removal. They get full-service restoration from a team who is personally invested in turning a nightmare into a bright, new beginning.

Which brings me to my next point:

How Does Your Work Impact the Lives of Your Customers?

If you're not sure what meaningful service your business offers the community, ask yourself:

> *"How does the service I provide impact individual lives?"*

For 911 Restoration, the answer is: We provide customers with a fresh start.

If you work in remodeling, you might usually think of yourself as someone who builds new kitchens, but the meaningful service you provide could be summed up as, "I fulfill dreams for homeowners."

When you choose to focus on how your business makes a lasting impact on the lives of your customers, it changes everything. It changes the way you market your services. It changes the way you interact with clients. It changes your customer service policies. And it changes the way you feel about your job, replacing desperation to survive with a more purpose-driven determination.

IN SHORT

- Find the meaning in your work.
- Center your business practices and your personal attitude around filling that need for your customers.

CHAPTER 5

Your Customers: Who and Why

Knowing your customer is as important as knowing your trade. I know that, as a tradesperson, it can seem like a job well done should be enough to make a business thrive. But remember, if you don't have customers, you don't have a business. And you aren't going to have customers if you don't know who they are and how to reach them.

No matter what you sell, you're not the only person selling it. Even if you provide a service that is absolutely essential, your buyers still have other options. And now with online platforms like Yelp and Google reviews, customers are likelier than ever to do some research before they decide how to spend their money.

Getting ahead in business means getting to know your customer so you can get on their radar and earn repeat business by fulfilling their needs.

Who are Your Customers?

As a business owner, it's important to know your customer persona so you know who you're selling to. That's Marketing 101, right? Know how your client talks, know how they think, and know where to find them.

What we talk about less often is how important it is to understand and empathize with your buyers when they're standing right in front of you. When you care about your clients—when you see who they truly are and what they're going through—they notice. And as a result:

- They give you their business.
- They become loyal customers.
- They become brand advocates, recommending your company to friends, family, and neighbors.

Now, any business owner who has spent time thinking about marketing knows to consider things like age, culture, education, and professional background when strategizing ad campaigns. These things are important, but in order to really make that strong, lasting connection, remember to ask yourself things like:

- *What problem does your customer have?* Don't just think about the surface problem; think about the deeper pain point. As the owner of a restoration company, I know my clients need property restoration, but the larger issue is that they need reassurance, guidance through a devastating problem, and the promise of a fresh start on the other side of disaster.

- *With that in mind, how do your customers see you?* What do you mean to them in this interaction? Are they looking for compassion? Authority? Answers?

- *What do they value personally?* Excellent service? Empathy? Direct, no-nonsense communication?

The more deeply you understand your clients, the better your shot at becoming their go-to champion.

Why are Your Customers Buying This Service?

This is another question that goes deeper than many business owners realize. Why are your customers buying this service to begin with?

For 911 Restoration, there's a pretty straightforward answer:

Our customers hire us because they've experienced property damage and they need someone to fix it.

But if we dig deeper, we can get to the heart of what they truly need and find the angle that helps us stand out among the competition. Let's try again.

Our customers hire us because the property they've worked so hard to build and maintain has been damaged or destroyed. They've lost their sense of refuge, they feel panicked, and they're hoping someone can make their home or business new again.

Do you see what I'm talking about? The way you engage with a customer who needs a mold inspection is going to be massively different from the way you engage with a customer who needs to know their family is safe from the health risks of a toxigenic infestation . . . even though it's the exact same customer. And that distinction marks the difference between a company that folds and a company that dominates the market.

How are Your Customers Finding Services Today?

Technology is constantly evolving. This means the way we seek out services changes every day. Even the way we shop for groceries is changing as there are now companies that deliver prepped meal ingredients right to our front doors.

As a business owner, you have to be on top of the changing trends. That doesn't mean you have to create a high-tech app specific to your business. Your target buyer might prefer to do things the old-fashioned way.

What I am saying is that you need to be aware of your customers' research and buying habits, today and into the future.

When buyers in the community seek out services like yours, where do they go? Do they ask friends and family for referrals? Do they search the Internet? Do they use online reviews to inform their buying decisions? Are there specific deals or promotions they search for? Do they pay attention to print ads in local publications?

Find the answers to these questions, and you'll be set to start finding the right customers in the right places.

IN SHORT

- Work to understand your customers on a deeper level.
- Recognize what core need has led them to seek out a service like yours in the first place.
- Find out how your customers find services like yours so you can tailor your marketing efforts.

CHAPTER 6

Getting Customers

So you've done all the work of getting to know your customers. The next question is: How are you going to bring them in?

To truly dig into marketing techniques, I'd have to write a whole other book. For now, I'll keep it simple and focus on the three major avenues for bringing in business.

Use Your Relationships

We prefer to do business with people we know and like.

That's just the truth about being human. Sure, you might skip out on your best friend's electrical services if he has a reputation for setting homes on fire, but all things being equal, we prefer to give our business to the people we know.

Use that. If you know anyone who might be able to use your services, reach out and let them know you're available. And if you have any news to share—a grand opening or new promotion—make an announcement even to the friends and acquaintances who don't seem like they'd have any reason to hire you. You never know when their situation will change or whether someone else will ask them for referrals.

Finding new customers is hard enough. While you do need to pursue the business of strangers, don't make things harder by neglecting the people in your inner circle who already trust you and want to see you succeed.

Online Lead Generation

A digital marketing strategy is imperative this day in age. Modern buyers turn to the Internet to find solutions for everything, and if you don't have a system in place for online lead generation, you are missing out on a lot of money.

The arena of online marketing is vast and complicated, so I'm not going to give you all the tools for your digital marketing strategy right here in this book. But just to get the wheels turning, some of the most reliable methods for online lead generation involve:

- An **SEO strategy** to make sure your website ranks near the top when customers search for services you provide
- **Pay-per-click advertising**
- **Content marketing**—blogs, videos, and infographics that establish you as an authority in your field
- Both **paid and organic social media marketing** to raise brand awareness and humanize your company
- **Email marketing** to keep customers informed about company news, promotions, referral programs, and anything else that keeps your business top of mind

You also want to make sure your company and contact information is correct in every directory where your business is listed, including Google and Yelp.

Referrals

Word of mouth. It's the oldest form of advertising and is still one of the most effective.

If you provide stellar service to a customer, you can bet that customer will—at the very least—recommend you to a friend or family member who needs that service later on down the road. Most likely, that recommendation will carry more weight than 100 Yelp reviews written by strangers.

But also remember that the reverse is true. If you provide shoddy service or one of your employees shows up with a rotten attitude, that customer's inner circle will find out about it. And the next time they're looking for a service you provide, they'll skip right on past your name, even if you're the first company listed in the search results.

So the first key to getting referrals is this: Give the kind of service customers will rave about.

My second recommendation is to find a way to pursue referrals actively. Don't hound your clients to sing your praises, but do encourage them to tell others if they were happy with their service. You might send a follow-up email with a link to your business's Yelp page so they can leave a review. Or maybe you can establish a referral program that rewards customers for sending someone else your way.

IN SHORT

- Make sure everyone you know is aware of your business and promotions.
- Invest some time, money, and employee talent in online lead generation.
- Encourage customers to give referrals ... and provide the kind of service that makes them *want* to recommend you to their friends.

CHAPTER 7

Closing Deals and Delivering Services

One of the most common mistakes I see business owners make is that when business is bad, they blame the marketing.

More often than not, the marketing is not the problem.

The problem is that they're not closing leads and they're not collecting money.

For the average tradesperson, the dream scenario would be to open a business, do a little advertising, provide great service, and rake in the profits. Most tradespeople enjoy doing skilled work; they're not wired for wheeling and dealing and they'd rather let their marketing do the heavy-lifting for them.

The problem is that, for most businesses, there are additional steps between the time when a customer learns that your company exists and the moment when they choose to buy your service. And those steps can make or break your business.

If your numbers are down and you can't figure out why, consider whether you're doing the following.

Make the Sale

Whether you prefer to deal with customers directly or you rely on staff to handle client relations, both you and your team need to know:

- What deeper service you're selling. (Chapter 4)
- How you add value to this customer's life or service experience.
- What problem you're solving.
- Why they should choose you over your competitor.

It becomes surprisingly easy to sell when you and your staff have these answers prepared and truly believe in the value of your service. Why? Because "making the sale" starts to feel more like an honest conversation about the work you do and less like making a pitch.

In my years as a business owner, I have learned that nobody likes to "be sold." But they do like to be assisted in making a purchase. What's the difference?

Think about the last time you went to a store with the intention of purchasing a gift for someone. When you walked into the store, did a sales associate just hand you an item and tell you to go to the register to pay for it? Of course not. They asked what you were looking for. When you told them you were looking for a Mother's Day gift, they followed up with questions like, "What are her hobbies? What movies or books does she like? What's her favorite color?" Then, they used your answer to make suggestions based on your mother's personal interests.

When you recognize this essential difference between selling and assisting, your so-called "sales pitch" turns into a conversation . . . which is far more effective and far more enjoyable for both you and the customer.

Delivering Service

If you're a tradesperson, you don't need me to convince you that consistently delivering excellent service is central to the success of a business. If you hold your staff and yourself to the highest professional standards, you increase your odds of getting repeat business and new referrals. In that regard, service is sales.

But here's something even the most skilled tradesperson can sometimes overlook:

> Service is not just about the quality of your work. It's also about how the customer feels throughout the interaction.

Every single time a buyer interacts with you or a team member, they are making a judgment about the quality of your customer service based on that experience. Which means every conversation you have with a customer is some form of sales pitch. Even if you're only answering a question about metered parking outside your storefront. The way you speak to them could make or break the sale.

I cannot tell you how many times a business owner has complained to me that business was slow because of the marketing. But then when I called their store, the receptionist was rude, disinterested, or unhelpful.

IN SHORT

Before you blame the marketing:

- Make sure you're closing a high percentage of your leads.
- Check the quality of service to see if you're giving customers a reason to stick around, come back, and sing your praises.

CHAPTER 8

Building a Team
and Culture

Now that you have a crystal clear vision for your business, you need to choose the players who are going to help you achieve that vision.

Hiring is both an exciting and intimidating undertaking for most entrepreneurs. Bringing other people on board for your mission opens up brand new possibilities, but it also comes with certain risks. A bad hire is ultimately a waste of salary and could cost you thousands of dollars in lost business. An outstanding hire can increase profits, boost the company's reputation, and improve morale.

With so much at stake, you can't afford to rush your hiring decisions. Before you post that "help wanted" ad, take some time to figure out what type of people you want on your team, what skill sets they should have, and what personality types best serve the company culture you hope to create.

Ask yourself:

Who Do You Need on Your Team and Why?

In Chapter 2, you took a good, hard look at the ways in which you can most effectively contribute to your business. You also determined the areas in which you need the most help. Look back at these answers to determine which roles you urgently need to fill within your company.

Consider:

- **What hiring decisions would free you up to focus on the work you do best?** Would hiring an office manager give you more time to do hands-on work for your clients? Or would having an additional tradesperson on your team allow you to spend more time on sales and business strategy?

- **What crucial skills are you currently lacking?** Do you have a hard time managing the books? Converting leads? Fielding customer questions or complaints?

- **What would it take to achieve the growth you want?** What does your dream business look like? How many tradespeople? How big is your sales or marketing team? Who do your clients turn to for customer support?

- **What are the expenses associated with the positions you'd like to fill?**

- **How much money do you have to invest in hiring at this time?**

- Considering your current needs, finances, and goals, **what are the most important positions to fill?**

Once you've answered these questions, dig a little deeper to determine which skills are most essential for each position. Know what you're looking for before you begin the hiring process so you can make decisions based on strategy and numbers; not based on moment-to-moment feelings.

Remember, you want to be *proactive*, not *reactive*.

Which brings us to the next crucial question . . .

How Will You Define Your Company Culture?

Building a team is not just about making sure all workplace responsibilities are covered. You also need to consider your ideal company culture.

What do I mean by "company culture?"

I'm talking about your work environment and team values. A culture develops naturally anytime you bring a group of people together. Their attitudes, the way they treat each other, the way they approach their work, the values they uphold . . . these elements define your company culture.

I've seen so many businesses struggle because the atmosphere and attitudes that shaped the company were not defined deliberately. At no point did the owner take the time to think about the culture they wanted to create. They just made a few hires based on skill sets alone and let their employees determine the work environment.

Don't let that happen to you. Take a moment now to consider the following questions:

- *What are your driving values as a business owner?*
- *What type of environment do you want to be in every day?*
- *How do you expect your employees to handle conflict?*
- *How do you expect your employees to treat each other? Management? The customer?*

- *When customers visit or call, how do you want them to perceive your company culture?*

Refer back to your answers as you make hiring decisions and develop company policy. Ask interview questions that help you determine if a candidate is a good personality fit for your company. Look for professionals who share your values. Design rules and guidelines that outline your company culture clearly so your employees understand what is expected of them in terms of behavior and attitude.

You may be in a hurry to get your business up and running, but trust me: you save more money in the long run if you take the time to determine exactly what you're looking for in an employee before you start passing out W-2s.

IN SHORT

- Decide which positions are most important to fill at this time.
- Focus on candidates who are skilled in your areas of weakness.
- Define your company culture before your employees define it for you.

CHAPTER 9

Management and Control

Now you know what you want out of this business. You know what success means to you, you know how you're going to make a name for yourself in the community, you know how you're going to make sales and deliver quality service. You even know who you're going to hire and how those professionals will contribute to your company culture.

In other words, you've got the Big Picture stuff figured out. Now comes the tough part.

How are you going to make the right business decisions day-to-day and into the future?

The concepts we're about to dive into may not be immediately obvious to you if you're coming from a trade background. Now that you're an entrepreneur, you have to take on an entirely new mindset and start seeing your business in terms of metrics, strategy, and measurable growth. If that sounds intimidating, stick with me. I'm going to walk you through the steps that help you take control and manage your company from the perspective of a business person.

Identify the Key Driver of Your Business

When I talk about "key drivers," I'm talking about the aspects of your business that drive the most growth. What assets are bringing in the most customers? What efforts are driving profits?

Your key drivers could be:

- Your sales team
- Your website
- Your referral program
- Competitive pricing
- A unique service that adds value for the customer
- Etc.

Determine the key business drivers for your company, and you'll find that important decisions suddenly become much easier to make. You'll know which assets to protect and where to invest your time, money, and resources going forward.

Measure Your Success

You can only improve what you measure.

> So always, always, *always* refer back to the metrics.

- How many leads did you get this month?
- How many of those leads did your team convert?
- How many jobs did you do?
- What was the average transaction per job?
- What were your profits?

When you have these answers at your fingertips, you can immediately see areas of weakness and opportunities for improvement.

You can also determine whether or not certain business decisions are paying off. Is the updated website generating more leads? Is the new sales hire closing those leads? The new rate increase improved your profit margin, but are you still booking as many jobs?

Without measurement, you're back to relying on your feelings. You wind up making knee-jerk decisions based on your bank account. You see less money coming so you decide the problem is the sales pitch or the pricing. In the end, you risk cutting out a key driver or investing money in the wrong problem.

Keep measuring your progress and let the numbers be your guide.

Stay in Control

The average business owner starts their company small. Extremely small. In many cases, it's a one-person operation. Maybe two or three at most. And when the business is that small, you know everything about it.

You know exactly how many sales you're closing, how many jobs you're doing, how much money you've collected, and which customer accounts are still not paid in full.

As your business grows, however, it can be all too easy to lose your grip on this information. You hire people to oversee sales and accounts receivable, and little by little, you stop checking in on the numbers . . . which means you no longer know how to manage, how to improve your business, and how to hold your team accountable so you can achieve growth.

No matter how much your business expands, stay in control of operations by staying informed. You should always know:

- How many leads you're getting
- How many projects you're taking on
- What your closing rates are
- Your total sales per week, per month, and per quarter

You also must set an annual budget and establish a routine to regularly review your Profit & Loss document, or P&L.

Your yearly budget should break down:

- Anticipated revenue
- Expenses such as payroll, marketing, office space, equipment, etc.
- Profits

Then, set a standing appointment each month to examine your P&L as it relates to this budget. Are you on track? Are you bringing in the kind of revenue you need? Is there any area where you need to pull back on expenses? And the bottom line: What is your profit, and how can you increase it?

If you leave it to your employees to oversee and interpret these numbers, you essentially give them control over your growth. I'll tell you this: Even if you have the most dedicated employees in the world, no one will ever care about this company as deeply and personally as you do.

Stay aware and stay in control.

Don't Just Grow Your Business; Scale Your Business

There is an important distinction between growing your business and scaling your business.

You can grow your business without scaling. This happens when you expand—add employees and increase transactions—but you don't actually see bigger profits. Your income and expenses increase at roughly the same rate.

Scaling is what happens when you increase income at a greater rate than expenses. For example, you streamline your systems to increase productivity and the number of transactions you are able to complete in a day without adding new expenses to your budget.

What we're talking about here is a classic tug-o-war for business owners. It would seem impossible boost profits without also hiring more employees, investing in more resources, and possibly even opening more locations. So how do you make sure you're continuously taking more money in than you're sending out?

Some of the most important practices for scaling include:

Establishing a standardized process for everything.
Make sure your employees have a consistent routine for following up with customers, recording sales, managing transactions, etc. Standardization equals efficiency, and efficiency means every minute is worth a little bit more.

Automating what you can.
While customer service will always require a human touch, look for the aspects of your business that can be made more affordable through automation. Can you create an option to book consultations online? Use SMS messaging to send reminders to clients?

Hiring the right people . . . and investing in them.
I just talked about this in Chapter 8, but it bears repeating: A good hire will save you money and bring in business. And if you've put together a team of driven, dedicated professionals, it may be worth it for you to invest in their growth with additional training and skill-building initiatives.

Being excellent.
Yes, this one is a little obvious, but it's also true. Do outstanding work, offer your customers something unique, rise above the competition, and you can get away with a small rate increase.

There are plenty of ways to scale your business, but the bottom line is to seek opportunities to increase efficiency, enhance team performance, and get a higher return for your efforts.

IN SHORT

The best practices for managing your company are:

- Know your key business drivers.
- Measure your success in numbers.
- Maintain control by staying informed.
- Focus your growth efforts on scaling your business.

CHAPTER TEN

Innovation

I t's only fair that I warn you: *As a business owner, you never truly "arrive."*

Hopefully, you do grow as a business. You build a bigger team, you reach your sales goals, and you expand your service area. But you should know that even if you meet your objectives, you can never sit back, relax, and call it a job well done.

Why?

> Because in order to survive in the long term,
> you must continually innovate.

Even as you accomplish your business goals, there is always a new competitor to beat or new technology to keep up with. There are always new challenges to overcome, which means your fulfillment as a business owner depends on 1) your ability to appreciate day-to-day growth and success and 2) your willingness to innovate.

What is Innovation, Really?

"Innovation" is such a buzzy term in the modern business world, it's come close to losing all meaning. The word is thrown around any time a company hopes to sound unique or a CEO wants to get more out of their employees.

So let me clarify in clear, practical terms what "innovation" should mean for you as an entrepreneur.

When you innovate, you:

- add more value
- much faster
- and at a better price.

Any change that allows you to do those three things amounts to "innovation."

Innovate or Die

You need to understand that innovation is not a luxury. It's not just the concern of high-end companies or saturated markets. You must continuously find ways to improve your process, products, and services no matter what industry you're in or where your business is located.

Why?

Because your competition is advancing all the time. They want to win, too, and they're always looking for new ways to serve customers better. Whether it's unveiling a new product, rebranding the company, making a service more convenient, or discovering a more affordable way to do business, the Other Guy is moving forward. And if you're sitting still, you're going out of business . . . even if you don't feel the effects of it yet.

Innovation is a Mindset

Many tradespeople struggle to make the shift to an innovation mindset. The skilled work you do is built on long-established systems and a universal understanding of what it means to provide quality service.

It's different in the business world.

A successful entrepreneur has trained his or her mind to constantly think in terms of innovation.

- *Where does my product or service fall short?*
- *How can I turn this negative review into a game-changing idea?*
- *That's a brilliant idea from the competition. How can I do better?*

If you don't naturally look for ways to innovate, start cultivating this mindset now. An easy way to do this is to start by looking at every obstacle as an opportunity to create a new solution . . . an opportunity to grow and become better. Little by little, you'll find that the innovative mindset becomes second nature, and your company will benefit from it.

Tools and Technology

One of the more intimidating aspects of innovation comes in the form of tools and technology. Whether it's a new machine to streamline work in the office or a new app for doing business, cutting edge tools have a way of making us feel overwhelmed and sometimes even incompetent.

This is where I remind you that it's your responsibility as a business owner to continually seek out opportunities to grow.

It's fine if you "hate technology." It's all right if, deep down, you "prefer the old ways." But it's also a mistake to let those personal preferences interfere with the ultimate success of your business.

Actively look for new tools that will make your business run more efficiently and make working with you more convenient for your customers. And when you come across technology that you know will help your business, bite the bullet and learn how to use it. These things get easier with practice. Watching your sales plummet only gets harder.

Innovation in Marketing

While you're looking for ways to improve your business, don't forget to look at your marketing.

Many business owners get stuck in a rut when it comes to customer outreach. They run the same print or pay-per-click ads for years. They do the same guesswork to determine how well those ads are paying off. They offer customers the same limited communication options.

The problem here is that the culture is evolving fast. Your competitors are finding new ways to engage with clients, and if you're still doing the same thing you've always done, you're bound to fall behind. Instead, look at these areas for opportunities to innovate:

- **How do you get in front of prospective customers?** Is your company easy to discover for the modern consumer, or do you need to invest more effort in social media marketing, video advertising, and other digital avenues?

- **How are you measuring your marketing success?** There are so many low-cost, digital marketing tools out there to help you track which ads and content lead buyers to your website and inspire them to convert. Learn how to use these tools so you can track your marketing ROI.

- **How are you communicating with clients?** Do they have multiple options for getting in contact with a company representative? How do they learn about new promotions? Perform a quick audit of your communication systems and see if you can make any aspect of customer relations more convenient with SMS messaging, email subscriptions, chat boxes, or any other new features.

Every day, the world moves forward a little bit more. And as your competitors innovate, your customer's expectations change. If you're not keeping up, you're losing.

IN SHORT

- Look for ways to add more value faster and at a better price.
- Make sure you're innovating beyond the competition.
- Cultivate an innovation mindset.
- Be open to learning new tools and technology.
- Update your marketing as well as your products and procedures.

Work on making these changes
a little bit every day, and I promise you:

You will be unstoppable.

CHAPTER 11

Success

The concept of "success" is complicated for a business owner. "Success" as we often think of it is a constantly moving target. We reach one goal and immediately shift our gaze to the next rung on the ladder.

I've talked a lot about using numbers and strategies to achieve financial success and tangible growth for your business. Now I'd like to touch on the attitudes and perspectives that help you experience a sense of accomplishment in this moment and set you up for excellence in the long run.

Because it isn't *all* about the balance sheet.

You see, when you focus on running your business in a way that upholds your personal values and emphasizes human connection, you offer your customers something no one else will. You offer meaningful, compassionate solutions. You become more than a quality company. You become a trusted resource within the community.

And not only does focusing on the big picture generate bigger profits, but it also allows you to discover a more meaningful definition of success for yourself. Running a business is hard. It can wear you down fast if you can't find appreciation and fulfillment in the day-to-day victories. When you open up your definition of success, you prevent burnout and enjoy deeper happiness in your career.

So, as you work towards growing your company, don't lose sight of the numbers. But don't lose sight of these less tangible objectives, either.

Fall in Love with the Process

Building a business is much more than creating a great product and putting it up for sale. In every part of the business and in every phase of growth, we face new challenges. In this moment, you might be trying to solve a cash flow problem or building a new team or improving your marketing campaigns. In the next moment, you'll be on to a brand new challenge.

When it comes to running a business, there is always a next thing, always a new mountain to climb. If you want to feel satisfied in your work, choose to appreciate the journey itself, because the destination is always moving.

It's actually easier than it sounds. Think of the last time you had a deeply enjoyable day at work. You may have gotten a raise or some recognition, but odds are that a large part of your satisfaction came from conquering a challenge or solving a problem alongside the colleagues you care about. It's fun to be a part of a team, and growth is always fulfilling.

Recognize these feelings now and as you move forward with your business.

Find the Meaning

I covered this subject in more detail in Chapter 4, but it's worth bringing up briefly now, because a meaningful career is a successful career. And a business that is designed to make the world better is a business that deserves your best efforts.

If you haven't done it yet, take a look at the role your company plays in your larger community. What important gift are you sharing? How are you making someone else's life easier, better, happier, or more complete because of the work you do?

Discover the deeper purpose behind your business, and you'll realize you've already succeeded in many ways.

Make a Connection

So much of our work satisfaction is determined by our ability to connect with other people. You not only improve others' lives through the work you do; you also link yourself to them in powerful ways.

Think of the last time you truly empathized with a customer's dilemma. Or the last client who shared exciting news from their personal life. Or even just the time you talked sports with a prospective buyer. Running a business offers you endless opportunities to connect with those in your community, and those connections create a sense of fulfillment and purpose on even the most mundane days.

Managing a company also allows you to develop unique relationships with your colleagues and employees. If you've successfully built a reliable and cohesive team (Chapter 8), you're set up to discover the deep satisfaction of working toward a common goal alongside people you care about. You and your staff . . . you're in this together. Your employees' challenges are *your* challenges and vice versa. When you embrace that exchange—when you choose to celebrate and uplift those around you—you experience a sense of completeness long before you attain your long-term business goals.

Focus on Growth

We've talked a lot about business growth in previous chapters. Now I want to talk about your own personal growth as a professional, as a human being, and as a team.

You know by now that you can expect to face a lot of obstacles as you build your business. These roadblocks can be frustrating, disheartening, and exhausting. And yet, somehow, these are also the experiences that enhance your sense of success.

At some point, we all learn that growth is what makes us happy. It's not the victory itself (although that's nice, too). It's not the things we achieve or the points we score. It's the experience of growing, adapting, and overcoming. It's the knowledge that we're building something, not just having success handed to us.

I meant what I said about measurable improvement. You do need to keep your eye on the metrics. You need to know exactly how many leads you're generating, how many leads you're converting, and what your profit margins are. This information shows you the way forward so you can overcome obstacles and reach the finish line.

But when you're longing to feel a sense of joy or personal accomplishment, lift your eyes from the numbers for a minute and look at the big picture.

IN SHORT

- Are you enjoying the process?
- Have you found meaning in your work?
- Are you connecting with customers and team members?
- Have you experienced consistent growth as individual?

If the answers to all these questions
is yes, then you're doing great.
The numbers will prove it in time.

Closing Thoughts

The only thing that stands between you and your goals is your perception . . . assuming you are ready to put in the hard work it takes to build your company. If you are passionate and invested, then it's probably your mindset that's holding you back. You're still leading with ego, "instinct," and fear instead of focusing on facts, numbers, and reality. You're viewing your business through the lense of a tradesperson-with-a-dream, not through the facts-focused eyes of an entrepreneur. I've seen so many new business owners make that mistake, including myself. I can tell you from personal experience that once you learn to get real with yourself and cultivate a growth mindset, you become better equipped with the strategies and solutions that have a meaningful impact on your company's growth.

In fact, that's really what this book is about—shifting your mindset to focus on the reality of your situation so you can make smart decisions for your business.

In my own journey, I quickly realized that my inability to see objective reality was what prevented me from moving forward. I was reacting to challenges based on my fears or my hopes or a hunch. I wasn't looking at the metrics. I wasn't turning inward to evaluate my own strengths and opportunities for growth. I wasn't thinking about the most strategic approach to building an accomplished company.

In other words, I didn't recognize how much control I had over my own success.

911 Restoration has since grown into a recognized, nationwide franchise because I learned to be honest with myself. I learned to evaluate my own skills truthfully, to humbly learn and improve, and to recognize and invest in the talents of my team members. I took a critical eye to my business, measured company performance in quantifiable terms, and sought the help I needed when I pinpointed weaknesses I couldn't fix on my own.

In short, I learned to lead from the perspective of a businessman. And if I could go from working the land to calling the shots for a major restoration company, you can do the same.

Refer back to the lessons in this book whenever you come upon another obstacle you don't know how to conquer. Practice cultivating a business mindset daily.

With patience, diligence, and passion, you're bound to discover how much you're capable of.

www.ingramcontent.com/pod-product-compliance
Lightning Source LLC
Chambersburg PA
CBHW061153040426
42445CB00013B/1674